TAKING ACTION ON CLIMATE CHANGE

SWEPT AWAY
Escalating Storms and Disasters

ALEX DAVID

Cavendish Square
New York

Published in 2020 by Cavendish Square Publishing, LLC
243 5th Avenue, Suite 136, New York, NY 10016

First Edition

Library of Congress Cataloging-in-Publication Data

Names: David, Alex, 1983- author.
Title: Swept away : escalating storms and disasters / Alex David.
Description: First edition. | New York : Cavendish Square, 2020. | Series: Taking action on climate change | Includes bibliographical references and index.
Identifiers: LCCN 2019019508 (print) | LCCN 2019981150 (ebook) | ISBN 9781502652355 (library binding) | ISBN 9781502652348 (paperback) | ISBN 9781502652362 (ebook)
Subjects: LCSH: Climatic changes--Juvenile literature. | Storms--Juvenile literature. | Natural disasters--Juvenile literature.
Classification: LCC QC903.15 .D378 2020 (print) | LCC QC903.15 (ebook) | DDC 551.55/4--dc23
LC record available at https://lccn.loc.gov/2019019508
LC ebook record available at https://lccn.loc.gov/2019981150

Copy Editor: Nathan Heidelberger
Associate Art Director: Alan Sliwinski
Designer: Ginny Kemmerer
Production Coordinator: Karol Szymczuk
Photo Research: J8 Media

The photographs in this book are used by permission and through the courtesy of: Cover Tino Adi P/Shutterstock.com; p. 4 Joe Raedle/Getty Images; p. 8 Hitforsa/ Getty Images; p. 11 Peter Newark American Pictures/Bridgeman Images; p. 13 Spencer Sutton/Science Source; p. 14 Jung Yeon-Je/AFP/Getty Images; p. 17 Fabrice Coffrini/AFP/Getty Images; p. 20 European Parliament from EU/Wikimedia Commons/File:Greta Thunberg at the Parliament (46705842855).jpg/CC BY-SA 2.0; p. 22 Kyle Niemi/U.S. Coast Guard/Getty Images; p. 25 Social Media/Reuters/Newscom; p. 27 Joe Raedle/Getty Images; p. 31 Courtesy of Paul Kucera/University Corporation for Atmospheric Research (UCAR)/3D-PAWS is supported by USAID; pp. 32, 36 NASA; p. 38 Patrick Lynch/Alamy Stock Photo; p. 40 Texas Pixel Pro/iStockphoto.com; p. 43 Mark Ralston/AFP/Getty Images; p. 45 Steve Heap/Shutterstock.com; p. 47 Daniel J. Prostak/Wikimedia Commons/File:Hunter's Point South Park – Phase 6 – Overlook.jpg/CC BY-SA 4.0; p. 48 Hanna Franzen/AFP/Getty Images; p. 50 Frances Roberts/Alamy Stock Photo; p. 51 Al Drago/Bloomberg/Getty Images;
p. 53 Jeffrey Greenberg/UIG/Getty Images; p. 54 Carolyn Cole/Los Angeles Times/Getty Images.

Printed in the United States of America

Portions of this book originally appeared in *Adapting to Intense Storms* by Adam Furgang.

CONTENTS

These homes in Puerto Rico were destroyed by Hurricane Maria in 2017.

Introduction

Beatriz Rodriguez wiped tears from her eyes and said, "We have to have patience. Stay united … My island had never gone through this." Rodriguez was referring to Hurricane Maria, which ripped through the small island of Puerto Rico, a territory of the United States, on September 20, 2017.

Hurricane Maria

In the fall of 2017, meteorologists anxiously tracked the weather system. On September 13, the National Hurricane Center saw a low pressure system move from east to west in the tropical Atlantic Ocean. At 6:15 a.m. on Wednesday, September 20, Hurricane Maria made landfall. Winds gusted at 155 miles per hour (249 kilometers per hour). Rain deluged Puerto Rico. The storm wiped out electricity all over the island. Some towns lost 90 percent of their structures. As the storm hit, meteorologists realized the winds had knocked out the National Weather Service's sensors. They had to rely only on satellites to track the storm.

During the storm, Beatriz Rodriguez's grandchildren, Samiliz and Mizraim, hid in their parents' bathroom. Although they made it through the storm, their parents decided that they should live in Florida with Beatriz, rather than stay in Puerto Rico. Many of the schools in Puerto Rico were unable to reopen after Hurricane Maria hit, but the children needed to go to school. Therefore, a month later, the children arrived at an airport in Florida. When they saw the fluorescent lights in the airport, the lights looked unfamiliar. The children had been living without electricity for almost a month. They would stay with their grandmother indefinitely, unable to return to their island until its infrastructure was fixed.

Tourists Affected

American tourist Joe Serrano was staying at a hotel in San Juan when Hurricane Maria hit. The hotel boarded up all windows and asked everyone to come to the main lobby. The vacationers could only bring linens. They all waited together as the storm passed through San Juan. They heard trees snap and wind whistling. Parts of the hotel ceiling fell down. They used pool water to wash their clothes and flush toilets. The electricity went out, and the guests had to rely on spotty generators to power their phones so they could send messages to loved ones. After the storm, Serrano walked the streets of San Juan, completely in awe of the damage. He took many photos, but the one he likes best was of the Puerto Rican flag. Written in red spray paint were the words "Together as One."

Catastrophic Event

This sense of unity is common among stories of Hurricane Maria. Tricia Wachtendorf, a professor of sociology at the University of Delaware, says Hurricane Maria had elements of a "catastrophic event." Less common than disasters, catastrophic events wipe out large amounts of infrastructure. Many man-made parts of communities that residents built, like buildings and roadways, were wiped away on September 20. The island was left largely to deal with the disaster itself. President Donald Trump and other members of the US government took six days before holding a meeting to discuss the impact of Hurricane Maria.

It is no wonder that unity is a large theme of these survivor stories. Together we can weather storms. Together we can predict and evacuate. Together we can investigate why such apocalyptic storms are happening now. Is it because of global warming? Are humans responsible for the increasingly devastating storms that are happening all over the world? We will investigate the connection between climate change and storms, define different types of storms, and see how we as individuals may learn from one another to create change that may bring calm to our wild weather.

This painting depicts the wild feeling of storms.

CHAPTER 1

The Cause and Effects of Global Warming

Professor Kerry Emanuel, an atmospheric scientist from the Massachusetts Institute of Technology, states that because of global warming, there is a "50-percent increase in the destructive potential of the most powerful tropical storms." However, he is resistant to making a direct correlation between global warming and any one storm. He says, "My feeling is, when there's a hurricane, there's an occasion to talk about the subject … But attributing a particular [weather] event to anything, whether it's climate change or anything else, is a badly posed question, really." Kerry points out what many atmospheric scientists agree on. Although climate change is likely to increase the severity of storms and the likelihood that they will happen, it's difficult to attribute global warming and climate change as the cause for individual weather events.

Global warming does make ocean and air temperatures warmer and therefore allows more moisture to be available for hurricanes, monsoons, and other extreme weather events. Although scientists don't have the data to understand if storms in the twenty-first century are a direct result of global warming, they can show that global warming is changing overall weather patterns and that climate change is largely due to human consumption of carbon.

Human-Caused Global Warming

The rapid increase in global surface temperatures began at the same time that the Industrial Revolution was getting under way. The rise has been in direct proportion to the increase in industrialized activities, which are heavily dependent upon the burning of fossil fuels. At the start of the Industrial Revolution at the end of the eighteenth century, nations such as Great Britain and the United States began using machinery to get work done. They relied more and more heavily on machines in the years that followed. They used steam power for trains, built factories that manufactured goods, and allowed for the mass production of goods for an ever-increasing population.

Powering the Industrial Age required burning fossil fuels, such as coal, oil, and gas. In order to get factories and machines to run, lots of power had to be generated. The burning of coal

Cars, now common on America's roads, contribute to humans' large carbon footprint.

was one way to provide the energy needed to make factories run, heat homes and businesses, and provide electrical power to large numbers of people.

When cars began to be manufactured on assembly lines in the United States, people all over the country were suddenly able to buy them at more affordable prices. All of those cars needed gasoline to make them run. As a result, more fossil fuels were extracted from the ground, refined into gasoline, and burned in large quantities in the cars' combustion engines. When fossil fuels are burned to power factories and provide heat and electricity to homes, pollution escapes into the air.

Similarly, when a car consumes gasoline, fumes are released into the air from the exhaust pipe.

Despite growing amounts of research about pollution, by the turn of the twenty-first century, fossil-fuel burning and the resulting carbon-based, heat-trapping emissions continued to increase. Today, many North American families have more than one car. Automobile use is becoming common even in underdeveloped countries where cars were once rare luxury goods.

The Greenhouse Effect

The release of greenhouse gases, specifically carbon dioxide, into the atmosphere is the crux of the problem that causes climate change. Carbon dioxide by itself is not a dangerous gas. In fact, you breathe it out with every exhalation of breath. Plants require carbon dioxide for respiration, and humans require the oxygen produced by plants as an end product of this process. The components that make up greenhouse gases on Earth include water vapor, carbon dioxide, methane, and ozone.

A phenomenon known as the greenhouse effect occurs when the sun's heat becomes trapped in the lower portion of the atmosphere, near Earth's surface. This effect is an ordinarily beneficial phenomenon that keeps Earth's atmosphere from losing too much of the sun's heat and becoming too cold to support life. However, the additional greenhouse gases that humans produce trap too much heat, cause an overall rise in

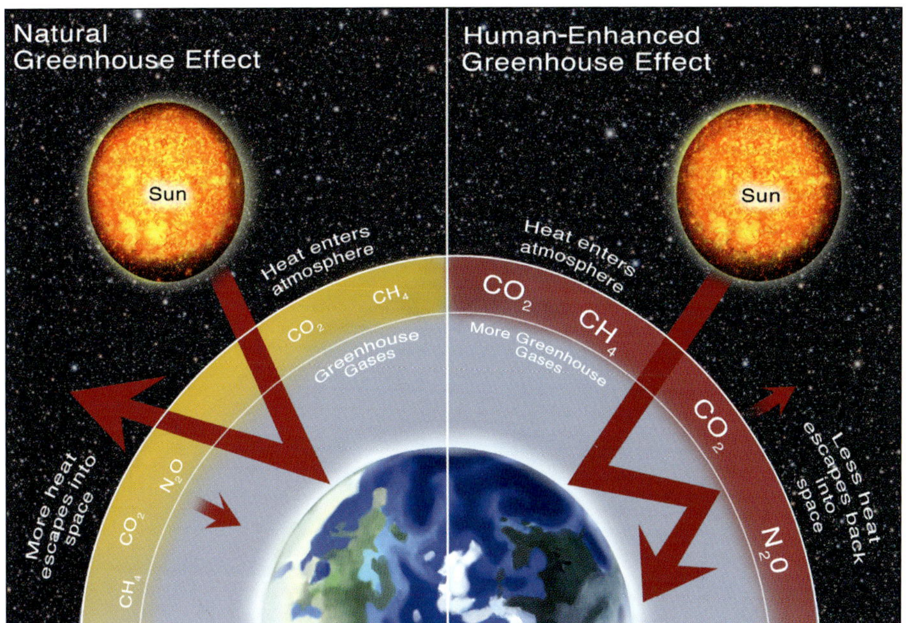

This diagram compares a natural greenhouse effect with a human-enhanced one: more heat stays in the atmosphere with the human version.

temperatures. It's the massive increase in the production and accumulation of carbon dioxide due to industrialization that is leading to rising temperatures and climate change.

Global Initiatives to Limit Greenhouse Gases

Since 1992, environmental and political leaders have been trying to decrease the greenhouse gases in the atmosphere. The Earth Summit in Rio de Janeiro was an important effort to get leaders of various countries to agree to limit their nations' greenhouse gas emissions. Since then, several nations have voluntarily reduced their emissions of the most dangerous

The forty-eighth session of the Intergovernmental Panel on Climate Change was held in South Korea in 2018 to exchange climate information.

greenhouse gases: carbon dioxide, methane, nitrous oxide, and sulfur hexafluoride.

The Intergovernmental Panel on Climate Change (IPCC), a panel set up by the World Meteorological Organization (WMO) and the United Nations Environment Program, is also vital to collecting research from scientists around the world and sharing it. Scientific collaboration and distribution of knowledge occurs when the IPCC holds climate meetings. In 2018, South Korea hosted the forty-eighth IPCC meeting. That year, the IPCC created a special report that addressed what will happen to the planet if it warms 2.7 degrees Fahrenheit (1.5 degrees Celsius) above pre-industrial levels. The report indicates that Earth is likely to reach 2.7°F (1.5°C) of warming between 2030 and 2052 if the planet continues to heat as it has been.

In order to understand how weather patterns and events are being disrupted and intensified by climate change and global warming, we must first start by examining how scientists collect data to make inferences.

NAMING THE STORMS

The National Hurricane Center began naming tropical storms in 1953. Before 1953, meteorologists used to name storms by the order they occurred and the year. This, however, became too confusing, and it was decided that giving the storms human names would be an easier way to report on them. At first, they gave all storms female names, but that changed in 1978. Now, the World Meteorological Organization follows a certain procedure for naming storms. They have premade lists for each year and each region of the ocean. In the beginning of the year, they start with "A" and then continue down the list. Each name alternates between being a male or female name. The lists are recycled every six years, unless a storm is so powerful and destructive that it would be insensitive to call another hurricane by the same name. In these cases, the name is retired.

Climate Models

Since the 1950s, mathematical models have been able to represent seasonal patterns in the atmosphere. In the 1960s, computers were able to precisely chart the circulation of air over water and land. They were also able to account for increasing carbon emissions into the atmosphere, resulting in far more accurate climate models. By the 1980s, computer models were able to focus on specific areas of the globe, and the National Center for Atmospheric Research has been continuing to improve this technology.

Today, computer climate models can be quite complex. Although scientists state that mean temperatures around the world are increasing, a close look at the models shows that there are some areas of the world that have been experiencing decreasing surface temperatures. These kinds of local variations and discrepancies can make climate data confusing and difficult to explain. A poor understanding of the climate models and global climate patterns also allows climate-change skeptics to exploit the potential confusion and spread the message that there is no cause for alarm.

Data Collection

The data that the climate models are based on has been collected through the cooperation of 186 member states and six member territories. The WMO coordinates more than ten thousand manned and automatic surface weather stations,

Above is the sign for the United Nations World Meteorological Organization, which is based in Geneva, Switzerland.

one thousand upper-air stations, seven thousand ships, one hundred moored and one thousand drifting buoys, hundreds of weather radars, and over three thousand specially equipped commercial aircraft that measure key parameters of the atmosphere, land, and ocean surface every day. In addition, the WMO Observing System contains operational polar-orbiting and geostationary satellites and research and development environmental satellites that complement the ground-based global observations.

Based on the data continuously gathered by these stations, today's computer climate models are now able to predict how temperatures will change over the next decades and into the next century. The models can be adjusted to show what would happen if various greenhouse gases in the atmosphere decreased, increased, or remained the same.

Take, for example, an increase of 5.4°F (3°C). With such an increase, many places that are already considered to have warm climates would no longer be able to sustain life. Many species of plants and animals would become extinct. The increased temperatures would cause more frequent deadly storms and severe droughts, as well as a rise in sea levels when glaciers in the Northern Hemisphere melt away into the ocean. Flooding would affect our ability to grow and harvest food. Areas that are not used to certain types of severe weather would have to deal with their consequences. Tornadoes all around the world would be more common, and hurricanes outside of traditionally warm, tropical areas would also occur more frequently. All of this could lead to human suffering and death, food and water shortages, and mass migrations.

Climate Models Aren't as Convincing as Hoped

Most scientists agree that global warming and climate change are both real and observable phenomena, and that they are well under way. The effects of warming and climate change are already being felt, and they are almost certainly irreversible in the short term. Climate scientists have tried—with varying degrees of success—to use the data and models to persuade political leaders to make and enforce laws that would mandate sharp reductions in emissions of carbon-based, heat-trapping gases. However, despite all of the data-gathering and computer-driven calculations, the models are just that—models. They are not hard facts or surefire certainties. There has been an increasing debate over the accuracy of the models and their ability to predict real climate change.

Even though climate models can change based upon newly gathered data and shifting variables, the general trends in the predictions have remained fairly constant and are agreed upon by most scientists in the field. The current levels of greenhouse gases trapped in the atmosphere will remain there for a long time, with carbon dioxide, in particular, lingering for hundreds of years even if no more is added from this point forward. This is why reversing the effects of global warming is highly unlikely in the short term, even with drastic emission-cutting measures. Most climate models paint a similar picture—more warming will occur at the poles and in northern areas, and many areas will be left uninhabitable, requiring mass relocations of millions of people. Yet global warming experts have been met with skepticism and controversy ever since they began releasing the results of their climate models.

The issue of global warming has become a political issue. The scientific data implies that a drastic change has to be made in public policy, corporate practice, industrial activity, and consumer habits. In short, we have to radically alter the way we live,

Greta Thunberg, a young climate activist from Sweden, meets with European leaders to talk about climate change in 2019.

work, travel, and consume. Anyone who suggests that we must drastically change how we live our lives, what we drive, and how we run our businesses is bound to be met with scrutiny. These ideas will be challenged by critics and those who stand to lose money as new energy sources, consumer habits, and corporate practices are explored and adopted. Such changes are costly and can cause considerable economic and social disruptions and dislocations.

Another reason climate-change skeptics do not like the current prediction models is that they do not account for some events, such as volcanic eruptions, that have an overall cooling effect on the climate. Some people think that unknown variables such as this make the data inaccurate and our climatic future uncertain and unknowable.

Regardless of the way individual climate studies are interpreted or the political maneuvering that drives competing claims regarding global warming, a large number of people—including the vast majority of climate scientists—agree that the climate does seem to be changing. There are more frequent and intense storms and weather events. There are more floods and droughts worldwide, they are occurring more often, and they are more severe.

Although we may not be able to convince people to make policy changes based solely on climate models, we can show data from events that have actually happened. If we look to the storms and disasters that have happened in the recent past, we may be able to show that climate change is something we need to care about. As Professor Emanuel stated, global warming has caused storms to become 50 percent more destructive. It is important to review the storms that have happened so that we may understand what our future climate will look like.

Hurricane Katrina damaged infrastructure in New Orleans, Louisiana, in 2005.

CHAPTER 2

Types of Storms

Humans often marvel at the power of storms. In Taino, a Native American language, the word *hurakán* was linked to a god of chaos. Storms are often associated with a menacing or evil force. It is no wonder that thunder and massive amounts of rain quicken the heartbeat of many of us, as we wonder if we will be safe. By looking at the types of storms that have already occurred, we can understand how climate change may be influencing the intensity and frequency of storms on Earth.

Thunderstorms

Most people have experienced thunderstorms. They are the most common form of severe weather. Thunderstorms occur when warm, moist air rises quickly. When this water vapor meets the cooler air above it, the vapor cools and condenses, forming clouds. Some of these clouds reach very high altitudes, and then water droplets fall as rain. Storms can often be accompanied by electrostatic discharges from clouds, called lightning. When the static discharge occurs, the surrounding air is heated quickly and intensely, causing the air to expand rapidly. This expansion of air as the result of lightning makes the sound known as thunder.

Thunderstorms most often occur in the afternoon, after the air has been heated all day. Some thunderstorms produce the type of cloud that could develop into a tornado. An increase in the overall temperature of Earth's atmosphere will cause thunderstorms to form more frequently, and the damage done by the storms will be more apparent and more costly.

Tornadoes

Tornadoes form most often in spring and summer, when the ground becomes warmer and the air above it is cooler. A tornado may form during a thunderstorm, when warm winds near the ground blow in one direction and cool air aloft blows in the opposite direction. The two masses of air begin to rotate. The warm, rising air that causes the thunderstorm pulls the rotating air mass so that it forms a vortex. This rotating air may cause a tornado if a funnel cloud connects the vortex to the ground.

Tornadoes can have wind speeds of more than 260 miles per hour (418 kmh) and can suck many objects into their path. Most tornadoes last just a few minutes and are a few hundred yards wide. A tornado destroys most things in its path, yet it can leave homes or other objects beyond its reach completely untouched.

Taylorville Tornado, 2018

In December of 2018, a tornado swept over 11 miles (18 kilometers) of land in Taylorville, Illinois. The tornado damaged 503 buildings, sometimes knocking bricks off of buildings and onto nearby cars. Twenty-six people were injured. The winds were over 155 miles per hour (249 kmh). This made the tornado an EF-3. Tornadoes are ranked using the Enhanced Fujita Scale. The scale goes from EF-0 to EF-5. An EF-3 tornado is considered a tornado that

A drone photo shows the damage done to Taylorville, Illinois, by a tornado in December 2018.

can cause severe damage. The Taylorville tornado was 0.5 mile (0.8 km) wide. Luckily, no one was killed in this tornado.

Hurricanes

Hurricanes start out as tropical storms over warm ocean waters. The warming waters of the Atlantic Ocean, the Gulf of Mexico, the Caribbean Sea, or the Northeast Pacific Ocean can cause what's generally known as a hurricane. Depending on their location, hurricanes can go by other names. They are called typhoons in the Northwest Pacific Ocean. In the Indian Ocean and near the ocean waters of Australia, they are called cyclones.

No matter what their name is, tropical storms occur when warm air at the surface of the ocean rises quickly. This rising air will soon meet up with cooler air above it, and the rising water vapor will cool and condense into storm clouds. As the clouds condense, heat is released, warming the air above the clouds. In turn, the clouds rise higher, making more room for humid air below the clouds.

The storm is slowly fed with moist air. The exchange of heat from the surface of the ocean to the atmosphere and back down again makes wind appear in a swirling pattern. The swirling pattern around the classic eye of the storm forms when winds near the surface of the ocean push together and water vapor is pushed upward, contributing further to the already circulating warm air. When the winds become greater than 74 miles per hour (119 kmh), the storm is upgraded from a tropical storm and is classified as a hurricane.

By the time hurricanes and tropical storms reach land, the winds have pushed the ocean water to well above normal levels. This temporary increase in sea level is called a storm surge. Some storm surges can be up to 25 to 30 feet (8 to 9 meters), causing massive flooding when they reach land. Hurricane winds are also extremely damaging. The strongest hurricanes can have wind speeds over 155 miles per hour (249 kmh), which is enough to destroy homes and create deadly flying debris.

Because they derive their energy from warm ocean waters, hurricanes and tropical storms tend to lose their strength as they

In 2018, Lisa Patrick returned to her destroyed Florida home to find all that was left after Hurricane Michael was a concrete slab.

move inland. However, the heavy rains that even downgraded hurricanes produce can cause massive flooding of rivers.

Hurricane Michael, 2018

In October of 2018, a category 5 hurricane—the most severe kind of hurricane—swept over the Florida Panhandle and made its way to Georgia. The storm, called Hurricane Michael, was the fourth most powerful hurricane to ever hit the United States at that time. It had winds of 160 miles per hour (257 kmh) and created a storm surge 9 to 14 feet (3 to 4 meters) high. It caused horrible damage to buildings and houses in Panama City Beach on the Gulf of Mexico. It blew the roofs off buildings, destroyed second floors of buildings, and even created two new inlets in St. Joseph Peninsula State Park on Cape San Blas. After the storm, cars could no longer reach part of the park because it was separated by water.

With the increased air temperatures associated with global warming, hurricanes form more frequently. In addition, the warmer air over the oceans can cause the hurricanes to increase in strength and wind speed, causing even greater damage when they finally make landfall.

Blizzards

Similar to a thunderstorm, a blizzard is caused when high and low pressure systems collide. Because the air is typically colder in winter, however, the resulting precipitation is snow instead of rain. Blizzards have winds of at least 35 miles per hour (56 kmh), causing little to no visibility because of the blowing snow. Blizzards can bring several feet of snow, take out power lines, and create conditions that are dangerous to drive in.

Some people have questioned whether or not an increase in winter weather events such as blizzards is a sign of climate change and global warming. Some people feel that an increase in snowstorms would seem to argue against global warming. However, an increase in all weather events—whether winter blizzards or summer tropical storms—would be consistent with the predictions of climate scientists. These researchers foresee an increase in precipitation and storminess for certain parts of the world due to a chain of factors that result from increasing air and ocean temperatures.

North American Blizzard, 2017

On February 8, 2017, the day before the blizzard struck, New York City and New Jersey had record warm temperatures. It was 63°F (17°C) in Central Park and 65°F (18°C) in Newark, New Jersey. Within twelve to fifteen hours, the temperatures sank by as much as 40°F (22°C). The snow piled in over Long Island, southern Connecticut, and the lower Hudson Valley. There were two thousand flight cancellations and many car accidents. There was even thundersnow, which is a frightening event featuring thunder and sometimes hail that occurs because of cold air mixing with shallow layers of air at about 20,000 feet (6,100 m).

3D-PRINTED AUTOMATIC WEATHER STATION (3D-PAWS)

3D-PAWS is an initiative by the University Corporation for Atmospheric Research and the US National Weather Service International Activities Office. It is a way to help expand meteorological networks that observe weather data. The weather stations are fairly cheap and easy to print. They take about one week to manufacture and cost about $200 to $400. If a component breaks down, it can easily be reprinted. The sensors on the weather stations can detect all sorts of weather data: wind speed, humidity, rainfall, and other variables.

Currently, 3D-PAWS is being utilized in the United States in Boulder, Colorado, and Sterling, Virginia, as well as in international locations like Kenya, Zambia, Barbados, and Curaçao. The stations are set up at schools and radio stations. Each station provides real-time weather data so meteorologists can predict storms better.

Here is a 3D-PAWS weather station, created through 3D printing.

As humans realize that all different types of storms are occurring, they must rely on meteorologists to let them know if they need to evacuate or how severe the storm will be. Meteorologists realize they need the most up-to-date ways to track storm systems so that they can tell people how to accurately respond to storms.

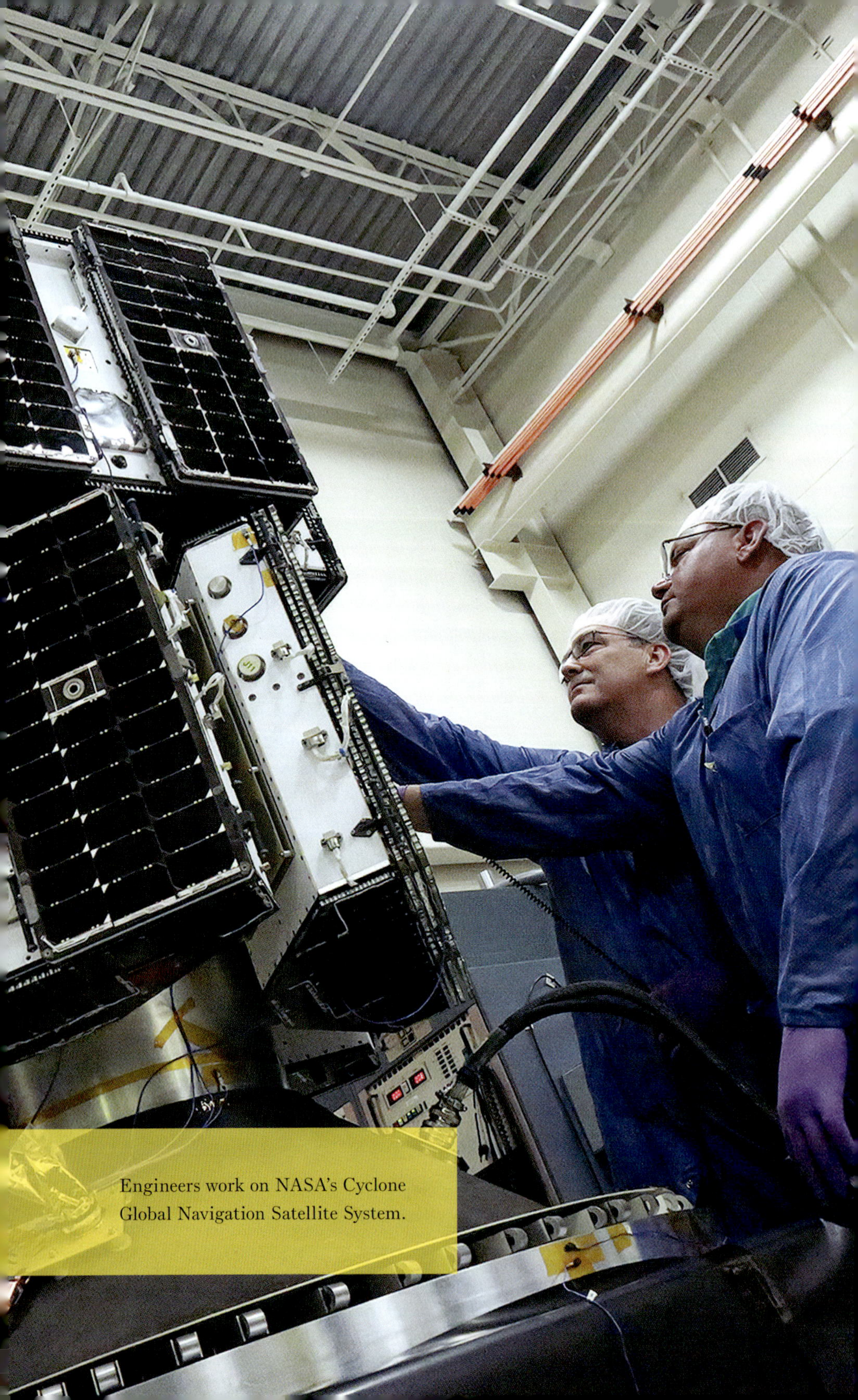

Engineers work on NASA's Cyclone Global Navigation Satellite System.

CHAPTER 3

Tracking Storms

To establish a relationship between storms and climate change, we would need to look at data for hundreds of years. However, we do not have this data. In the past, scientists relied on accounts of storms from sailors who were out on ships during rough weather. Storms that happened when there were not any ships around were not reported. Therefore, it is difficult to analyze long-term data concerning storms and climate change.

However, there are some clever ways that atmospheric scientists have started obtaining data about past and present weather. We started using satellites to track the weather in 1960. Additionally, meteorologists look to geology records to learn more about the past, using a field of science called paleotempestology. Physics can also be used to determine storm likelihood.

When people are warned of storms well ahead of time, they can take the necessary precautions to protect their homes from damage. They can also remove themselves from harm's way and possibly avoid injury or even death. Especially in coastal areas that are hit with frequent hurricanes, storm preparedness is an important way to adapt to a changing environment that encourages stronger and more frequent weather events.

Satellites

Modern satellite systems and radar help spot storms forming thousands of miles out to sea. Scientists can then track each storm's development and movements and warn people in the path of it to be prepared. Because of these advances in weather prediction and tracking, communicating storm-related news and warnings has become much better in recent years. Now, news stations provide alerts and warnings in enough time for people to prepare for coming storms. People can look on the internet to find satellite maps showing where a storm is currently located and where it is predicted to be in the next several hours or even days. Being prepared for the intense storms that will likely become more common with global warming is an important way for humans to adapt to the problem. When they see a strong and destructive storm coming, they can get out of the way of the destruction well ahead of time.

NASA's TRMM and GPM Satellites

In 1997, NASA launched the Tropical Rainfall Measuring Mission (TRMM) into space. Then, in 2014, it launched the Global Precipitation Measurement Mission (GPM) to replace the TRMM, which ceased operation the following year. These satellites have allowed scientists to track storms that have precipitation features, like thunderstorms. One scientist who has worked with the data is Dr. Chuntao Liu, from Texas A&M University.

Dr. Liu and other researchers were able to create a collection of precipitation features in a database based on the TRMM and GMP satellites. They could analyze the radar echoes to see what kind of precipitation was occurring. For instance, if they were to find 40 dBZ radar echoes in the upper levels of a cloud, where temperatures are below freezing, the scientists would know that graupel (soft hail) or hail would most likely be occurring. A process called riming takes places here. Riming is when very cold cloud droplets catch an ice particle and freeze around it. When this happens, graupel is formed. If the riming is very intense, hail can form. Dr. Liu and his colleagues were able to use the satellites and the radar echoes to determine where intense storms may occur. They found the Great Plains in the United States, central Africa, Pakistan, northwestern India, and southeastern South America to be "hot spots" for storms.

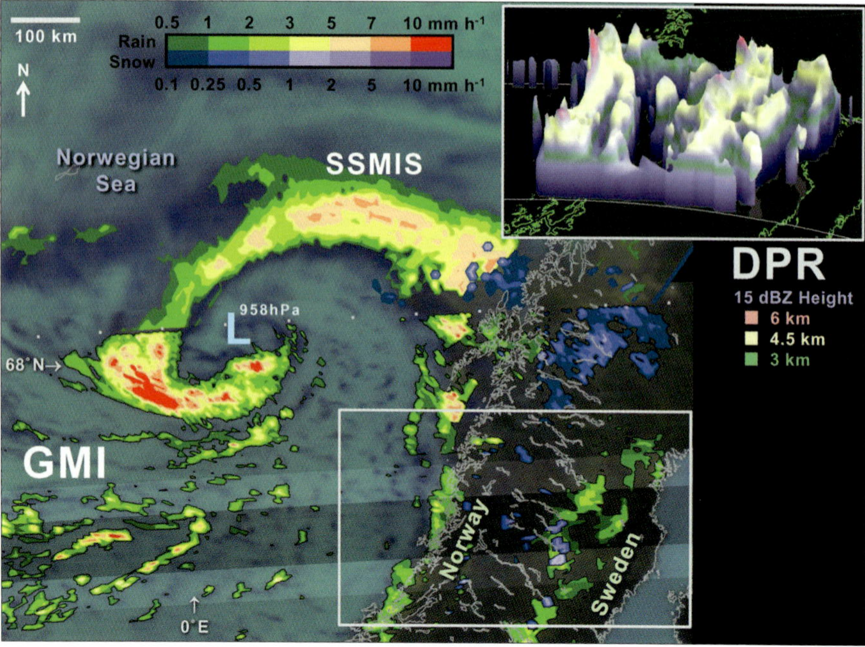

The data above is from a GPM satellite that tracked a storm that approached Norway in 2014.

CYGNSS Scatterometry

In the 1970s, NASA created a scatterometer that flew from NASA's Skylab. The device was able to measure surface ocean winds. In 2016, NASA launched the Cyclone Global Navigation Satellite System (CYGNSS). This was the most advanced scatterometer yet. It was able to detect winds in the eyewall of cyclones. Devices like this allow meteorologists to track storms in time to give people warnings.

Physics and Storm Prediction

Hurricanes are essentially large heat engines. They are able to take large amounts of heat energy from the sea and atmosphere and convert it into wind energy. A hurricane is so powerful that at its peak, one single hurricane may contain three thousand times the power of all the electricity generated on Earth. The hurricane is able to get its energy from water condensation. Think about it this way: It takes energy to boil water. The reverse is true for when water condenses, or turns from a gas to a liquid. When water condenses, it gives off energy. Atmospheric scientists

PALEOTEMPESTOLOGY

Atmospheric scientists have found that geology is an effective way to collect past storm data and make inferences about storms and climate change. The field of paleotempestology allows scientists to go to a marsh or swampland and take a core sample. They then analyze the core sample, using radiocarbon dating to date the layers of mud. Jeff Donnelly of the Woods Hole Oceanographic Institution (WHOI) takes graduate students out on canoes to take core samples from marshes. The theory is that when a hurricane hits a beach, sand is swept up over the beach and into nearby marshes. By measuring the data from these marshes, Donnelly and his team can learn a lot about storms from the past. They can identify hurricanes from hundreds of years ago. This is exactly the type of data that is needed to see what kind of connection exists between climate change and storms.

are able to use formulas for calculating max wind speed for storms and are then able to make predictions about the potential intensity of each storm. Physics, along with climate models, is helpful in predicting storms of the future. As more greenhouse gases go into the atmosphere, it can be inferred that there will be more storms and they will be more intense.

Saffir-Simpson Hurricane Wind Scale

The Saffir-Simpson Hurricane Wind Scale rates hurricanes based on their potential to do harm to people and property. For example, a category 1 hurricane with wind speeds from 74 to 95 miles per hour (119 to 153 kmh)—the least powerful type of hurricane—can create falling or flying debris that puts people, pets, and livestock at risk of injury and death. Mobile homes

In 2004, Hurricane Charley destroyed this mobile home park in Florida.

can experience damage to their roofing shingles and siding, even if they are anchored to the ground properly. Permanent homes may suffer damage to shingles, gutters, and chimneys.

A category 5 hurricane—the most severe type—can cause major damage. With winds in excess of 157 miles per hour (253 kmh), catastrophic damage can occur. People, pets, and livestock run a very high risk of injury or death from flying debris, even if they remain indoors. Mobile homes may be completely destroyed, regardless of how well they are built. A high percentage of permanent frame homes can be destroyed, with total failure of many roofs and walls. Power outages may last for weeks or even months, and water shortages are possible.

While we may not be able to eliminate the damage caused by category 5 hurricanes, it helps to understand the destructive potential the storms have and prepare for them as much as possible. With our current meteorological computer modeling and predictive technologies, we already know a lot about the behavior of hurricanes as they hit land. The information at our disposal includes a hurricane's wind speeds, its category rating on the Saffir-Simpson Scale, its approximate arrival time on land, and its likely path.

Satellite data, physics, geology, and historical records all allow scientists both to analyze the storms that have already happened and to warn people about storms that may occur. With advance notice, people can evacuate and find safe places while the storm takes its course.

In 2017, people evacuated as Hurricane Harvey approached Midlothian, Texas.

CHAPTER 4

Responding to and Preparing for Storms

There are many ways that people can respond to storms and prepare for the next one. From listening to the radio for alerts to evacuating when told to do so, people must be prepared to drop everything if a storm hits. Many times, people think they can stay in their houses during a storm. However, ignoring an evacuation order is not a good idea. In addition to immediately responding to storms, communities are learning from previous disasters. After a storm hits, architects are redesigning vulnerable spaces. Using innovative architecture, communities are figuring out how to provide spaces that are storm resistant. Therefore, when another storm hits, the damage won't be as brutal.

Storm Alert Systems

The National Weather Service, through its Storm Prediction Center (SPC), is able to warn people of dangerous thunderstorms and tornadoes. They can often let residents know up to eight days before a storm hits that severe weather is on the way to their area. The SPC uses sophisticated programs to warn people about dangerous weather.

One of these programs is called Convective Outlooks. It uses a number, a color, and descriptive labeling (like "moderate" or "high") to warn residents of approaching storms. Predicting threatening weather is not an exact science. The Convective Outlooks are called "subjective probabilities." The higher the number and the stronger the language, the higher the probability of a storm occurring in a given area. It's important to know the weather each day by listening to the radio, checking your computer or phone, or watching television. If there is a threat, it's a good idea to potentially change your plans for the day. Sometimes a threat is large enough that there will be an evacuation notice.

Evacuating

Governments tend to be cautious when considering evacuations. They know that an evacuation may be inconvenient, but it helps to minimize deaths, injuries, and post-storm rescue missions. Each storm that must be dealt with is serious, with evacuation considerations to be made about the elderly, the sick, and those residing in especially vulnerable areas. A plan must be put in place for how to organize and carry out large-scale evacuations and where to shelter those who must flee their homes.

When storm warnings are issued, the smartest thing for people to do is listen to and heed those warnings. They are meant to save lives and property, even if they require inconvenient responses, such as mandatory evacuation. The decision to call for an evacuation is not made lightly. It is done with great consideration for the safety of the community and an awareness of how disruptive the process can be for residents and business owners. People who choose to stay behind during storms may be risking the lives of first responders who could be sent in after them if trouble arises.

People affected by Hurricane Harvey in 2017 seek assistance from federal workers.

LIN-MANUEL MIRANDA

After Hurricane Maria hit Puerto Rico in 2017, *Hamilton* creator Lin-Manuel Miranda wrote a song, "Almost Like Praying," to raise donations for the Hispanic Federation Puerto Rico relief effort. He also brought *Hamilton* to San Juan for twenty-three performances on the Caribbean island. This effort raised $15 million for Puerto Rico. Oprah Winfrey was so inspired by Lin-Manuel Miranda's connection and dedication to the disaster-struck island that she donated $2 million to the Hispanic Federation and the Flamboyant Arts Fund. This shows that creativity in times of tragedy is a useful method of raising awareness and support for communities that are suffering.

Building for the Future

When buildings are constructed in tornado, hurricane, blizzard, or flood zones, special precautions are taken to make those homes and businesses as strong as possible. An EF-5 tornado on the Enhanced Fujita Tornado Scale, a category 5 hurricane on the Saffir-Simpson Hurricane Scale, or a river that has overflowed its banks can be a dangerous and even deadly event for the people in the area. In the future, these kinds of destructive events will likely be more widespread. Tornadoes will occur more frequently,

These coastal Californian homes are built on piles, which are columns that support structures.

and not only in Tornado Alley—the part of the central United States most often affected by these storms. Hurricanes will not only hit areas closest to the tropics. This means that building codes nationwide will need to be reviewed and revised in order to ensure that buildings are able to withstand various kinds of killer storms. The problem is that, realistically, not all older homes are going to be retrofitted with the latest storm-safety enhancements and technologies. The cost for most homeowners would be too great. While future homes will likely include the latest storm-proofing features and technologies, older homes will likely remain highly vulnerable to the destructive effects of intense storms.

In an attempt to address the high costs of retrofitting older homes and buildings, local, state, and federal governments are beginning to offer incentives to residents of storm-prone areas to stormproof their homes. These incentives take the form of tax credits, sales-tax holidays, and government grants. These home and building improvements will keep citizens safer, and they will cut down on insurance costs. Architects are also treating vulnerable coastal areas as problems that require innovative solutions. They see these storm-prone areas as an opportunity to use sustainable and innovative design techniques.

Hunter's Point South Waterfront Park

Standing in Hunter's Point South Waterfront Park, people may not realize they are in New York City. It is a prime example of function mixing with feng shui. The park is peaceful to look at and to be in. Artist Nobuho Nagasawa installed sculptures that represent the phases of the moon. There is a playground, lots of green space, and a tidal marsh that has native plants. However, Hunter's Point isn't designed just for relaxation but also for environmental resiliency. It was originally thought of in 2008 and then officially completed in 2013. It cost $105 million but saved about $30,000 between 2014 to 2017 because the park can actually generate electricity. In 2012, the park was able to accommodate the 4-foot (1.2 m) surge of Hurricane Sandy. It was not destroyed and actually was built to help when intense

At Hunter's Point South Waterfront Park, artist Nobuho Nagasawa created *Luminescence*, a set of sculptures representing the phases of the moon.

storms exactly like Hurricane Sandy roll in from the Atlantic. It allows for a 6-foot (1.8 m) storm surge, and if the East River floods, it can hold 557,800 gallons (2.1 million liters) of water. The park exemplifies the kind of architectural thinking that is needed for the future.

Realistically, humans must be prepared for future storms. They could be more intense and occur more often than before. Humans must build cities in new ways. They must know the weather and be prepared to change if conditions are unsafe. In addition to adjusting to more storms, there are many ways we can be the change that lessens climate change.

Activist Greta Thunberg holds a sign that says "School Strike for the Climate" outside the Swedish parliament building in 2018.

CHAPTER 5

Be the Change

As you read this book, you may feel powerless. How can ordinary citizens create any kind of change? Aren't policies decided by adults? Yes, but climate change movements are gaining momentum with young people. Young people are the force behind many successful demonstrations. All over the world, kids are protesting. They are following young people like Greta Thunberg and are asking adults to make better decisions in regard to climate policy. There are so many things that you, as a young person, can do to influence your community.

Local, State, and National Action

On the local level, you can be most helpful by providing help to your community after damaging weather events. Find out how to donate to or volunteer for a local chapter of the American Red Cross or other nonprofit or charity organizations that help those in need. It is a great way to provide help for your neighbors after an emergency. After a storm, communities and towns may be left without electricity or clean water. They need donations from the community to help them get back on their feet. Organizations sometimes take contributions of food, water, clean clothing, toiletries, or anything else that can be spared for people who are trying to get back on their feet and rebuild their lives.

Volunteering to help clean up after severe weather events is an excellent way to get involved and make a difference. Make sure you sign up with a responsible adult who can work alongside

Two volunteers clean up after Hurricane Sandy in 2012.

Representative Alexandria Ocasio-Cortez speaks in 2019 about her proposed Green New Deal to combat climate change.

you and keep you safe while helping out in possibly hazardous conditions. Local scouting and student volunteer groups can also work together to assist and clean up a storm-ravaged community. Searching online is a good way to find out about some of these community-minded organizations.

At the state level, you can get involved with groups that promote environmental protection and awareness, lobby state lawmakers, and influence state policy. Just as each nation can pledge to reduce its carbon output by a certain amount each year, so can states. Citizens' opinions and actions regarding carbon emissions and environmental protection have a definite influence on representatives in state government.

When supporting and choosing a national leader, it is important to know his or her stand on environmental issues. A

GRETA THUNBERG NOMINATED FOR NOBEL PEACE PRIZE

Sixteen-year-old Greta Thunberg, a student from Sweden, was nominated for the Nobel Peace Prize in March of 2019. The youngest person to ever receive the prize is Malala Yousafzai of Pakistan, who won the prize when she was seventeen years old.

Thunberg was nominated because of her good work in protesting climate change. A changing climate may mean a more hostile and less peaceful world, as food and water shortages are likely to increase wars. Thunberg has launched an international movement for young people called "Fridays for the Future." You can find Thunberg's movement, and even join a protest yourself, by looking up the Twitter hashtag #FridaysforFuture.

president's or congressperson's environmental philosophy will have an enormous impact upon federal policies and laws, both during and potentially far beyond his or her time in office.

Habit Change

Apart from political action, citizens can do a lot individually and collectively to cut down on the output of greenhouse gases.

Ordinary people do not have to wait for governments or industries to take the lead; they can take action immediately by choosing energy sources that do not rely on burning fossil fuels. When we pollute less, we help protect and heal the environment. By using solar- or wind-powered energy methods, we can avoid putting heat-trapping greenhouse gases into the atmosphere.

Taking care not to waste energy is also a good way to help the environment and reduce carbon emissions. Today's world population is about seven billion people. Just fifty years ago, it was three billion. As the world's population has exploded, its energy needs and reliance on fossil fuels have exploded too. This increase in population and energy consumption only contributes to a warming atmosphere and related climate change. If billions of humans are going to be able to continue living on this planet, with adequate food and water supplies and a climate that fosters life, they are going to have to embrace clean energy sources. They must also radically reduce the amount of greenhouse gases emitted into and collecting in the atmosphere.

Consider riding your bike instead of driving a car as a means to help the planet.

Together as One

Storms that are both more frequent and more intense are

A tattered Puerto Rican flag reads "Together as One" after Hurricane Maria.

a likely future reality. It is only by thinking and acting as a community—a community of global citizens—that we will successfully adapt to climate change and hopefully begin to reverse its worst effects. The days of selfish, individualistic action and wasteful and careless consumption are over. We must all come together and share the sacrifices and work as a global community of brothers and sisters. We must all join forces to secure our planet—the only home and shelter we humans have—against the ravages of past human activity. We must turn our gaze toward tomorrow and change our habits and practices in order to guarantee a place for human life in the planet's future.

Just as the stories from Hurricane Maria emphasize the importance of unity, we must rally together in order to help keep our Earth healthy. We must look out for not just our generation but also the generations of people who will come after us and inherit this planet. It is our responsibility now to limit the storms that may come as a result of increased global warming. When we come together and collectively share our knowledge, change our habits, redesign our architecture, and improve our responses, we are more powerful than when we act alone.

Glossary

carbon dioxide A greenhouse gas naturally present in the air but also produced by the burning of fossil fuels.

climate change A long-term change in Earth's climate, usually seen as a result of human activity.

climate model A computer simulation that predicts future climate conditions over a specific period of time.

correlation A relationship between two variables.

cyclone Another name for a hurricane, used to describe storms in the Indian Ocean and around Australia.

Enhanced Fujita Tornado Scale A rating system that categorizes the strength of tornado winds on a scale of 0 to 5, with 5 being the strongest.

fossil fuel A type of fuel that is from plant or animal remains, such as natural gas, coal, or oil.

global warming A significant and sustained increase in global surface and ocean temperatures; a consequence of human activity (such as the burning of fossil fuels) and the buildup of heat-trapping carbon emissions and other greenhouse gases in the atmosphere.

graupel Soft hail or pellets of snow.

greenhouse effect The trapping of the sun's warmth in Earth's lower atmosphere.

greenhouse gas A gas that contributes to the greenhouse effect, such as carbon dioxide or methane.

hurricane A storm that forms over the ocean with wind speeds over 74 miles per hour (119 kmh).

inference An opinion based on a fact or facts.

monsoon A period of heavy rainfall in India and other nearby areas.

paleotempestology A field of study that uses geological evidence to identify past storms.

riming The process of supercooled water droplets freezing into ice crystals.

Saffir-Simpson Hurricane Scale A rating system that categorizes hurricane wind strength on a scale of 1 to 5, with 5 being the strongest.

scatterometer A satellite instrument which uses radar to measure wind speeds.

tropical storm A storm that forms over the ocean with winds between 39 and 73 miles per hour (63 and 118 kmh). If the wind speed increases beyond that range, the storm is considered a hurricane.

typhoon A tropical storm or hurricane that forms in the Northwestern Pacific Ocean.

Further Information

Books

Barnett, Cynthia. *Rain: A Natural and Cultural History*. New York, NY: Penguin Random House, 2015.

Fies, Brian. *A Fire Story*. New York, NY: Abrams ComicArts, 2019.

Herbert, Megan, and Michael E. Mann. *The Tantrum That Saved the World*. Amsterdam, Netherlands: World Saving Books, 2017.

Machajewski, Sarah. *Weather and Climate Around the World*. New York, NY: PowerKids Press, 2019.

Metcalf, Gilbert E. *Paying for Pollution: Why a Carbon Tax Is Good for America*. New York, NY: Oxford University Press, 2019.

New York Times Editorial Staff. *Climate Refugees: How Climate Change Is Displacing Millions*. New York, NY: New York Times Educational Publishing in association with The Rosen Publishing Group, 2019.

Websites

MIT's Earth, Atmospheric and Planetary Sciences Department
https://eapsweb.mit.edu
Readers can stay up-to-date about climate change through the articles and free online courses on MIT's website.

NASA's Precipitation Measurement Mission
https://pmm.nasa.gov/precipitation-measurement-missions
Visitors to this site can read about the latest scientific technology for tracking storms.

3D-PAWS Weather Stations
https://www.iepas.ucar.edu/core-programs/3dpaws
3D-printed weather stations all over the world can be tracked using the map on this website. Readers can also learn about the 3D-printing process.

Organizations

Federal Emergency Management Agency (FEMA)
500 C Street SW
Washington, DC 20472
(202) 646-2500
Website: http://www.fema.gov
FEMA is a division of the US Department of Homeland Security and supports first responders and citizens who have been endangered by disasters such as severe weather events.

Indigenous Environmental Network
PO Box 485
Bemidji, MN 56619
(218) 751-4967
Website: http://www.ienearth.org
Using indigenous knowledge and natural law, the Indigenous Environmental Network seeks to protect the planet. Their website allows readers to learn about current climate events and topics.

National Hurricane Center
11691 SW 17th Street
Miami, FL 33165
(305) 229-4470
Website: https://www.nhc.noaa.gov/aboutintro.shtml
Located at Florida International University, the National Hurricane Center seeks to lessen the damages caused by hurricanes by providing the public with hurricane alerts.

National Weather Service
1325 East West Highway
Silver Spring, MD 20910
(828) 271-4800
Website: https://www.weather.gov
The National Weather Service helps inform the public about weather-related emergencies.

People and Planet
PO Box 21006
RPO Ottawa South
Ottawa, ON, Canada
K1S 5N1
(613) 744-3392
Website: http://www.planetfriendly.net
People and Planet lists jobs, volunteer positions, and guides that relate to the environment.

350.org
20 Jay Street
Suite 732
Brooklyn, NY 11201
(646) 801-0759
Website: https://350.org
350.org is a website that allows climate activists to unite and network so that they may organize protests around the world.

World Meteorological Organization
7bis, Avenue de la Paix,
Case Postale 2300
CH-1211 Geneva 2
Switzerland
Email: wmo@wmo.int
Website: https://public.wmo.int/en
This website is a source for readers to find out about climate initiatives and news.

Selected Bibliography

Ahrens, C. Donald, and Perry J. Samson. *Extreme Weather and Climate*. Belmont, CA: Brooks/Cole, 2010.

Biello, David. "Can Climate Models Predict Global Warming's Direct Effect in Your City?" *Scientific American*, March 23, 2010. http://www.scientificamerican.com/article.cfm?id=climate-models-predict-global-warming-effects-in-cities.

Burt, Christopher C. *Extreme Weather: A Guide and Record Book*. New York: W. W. Norton & Co., 2007.

Congressional Budget Office. *Potential Impacts of Climate Change in the United States*. Washington, DC: Congressional Budget Office, 2009.

Cullen, Heidi. *The Weather of the Future: Heat Waves, Extreme Storms, and Other Scenes from a Climate-Changed Planet*. New York, NY: Harper, 2010.

Gore, Al. *Our Choice: A Plan to Solve the Climate Crisis*. Emmaus, PA: Rodale, 2009.

Hoggan, James. *Climate Cover-Up: The Crusade to Deny Global Warming*. Vancouver, BC, Canada: Greystone Books, 2009.

Hollingshead, Mike, and Eric Nguyen. *Adventures in Tornado Alley: The Storm Chasers*. London, UK: Thames & Hudson, 2008.

Kahl, Jonathan D. W. *National Audubon Society First Field Guide: Weather*. New York, NY: Scholastic Reference, 1998.

"Kerry Emanuel on Climate Change and Hurricanes." Open Matters, August 29, 2017. https://mitopencourseware.wordpress.com/2017/08/29/kerry-emanuel-on-climate-change-and-hurricanes.

Lim, Eunjung. "South Korea Hosted the 48th IPCC Meeting." Climate Scorecard, November 28, 2018. https://www.climatescorecard.org/2018/11/south-korea-hosted-the-48th-ipcc-meeting.

Mogil, H. Michael. *Extreme Weather: Understanding the Science of Hurricanes, Tornadoes, Floods, Heat Waves, Snow Storms, Global Warming, and Other Atmospheric Disturbances*. New York, NY: Black Dog & Leventhal Publishers, 2007.

Murphy, Barb. "Cutting Edge Technology to Combat Climate Change." National Academies Press. Retrieved September 4, 2011. http://notes.nap.edu/2010/11/02/cutting-edge-technology-to-combat-climate-change.

Ocasio, Bianca Padró. "Displaced by Hurricane Maria, Puerto Rican Children Trace New Path in Central Florida." *Orlando Sentinel*, April 6, 2019. https://www.orlandosentinel.com/weather/hurricane/puerto-rico-hurricane-recovery/os-puerto-rico-students-moving-central-florida-20171012-story.html.

"Saffir-Simpson Hurricane Wind Scale." National Hurricane Center. Retrieved May 2019. http://www.nhc.noaa.gov/sshws.shtml.

Schneider, Bonnie. *Extreme Weather: A Guide to Surviving Flash Floods, Tornadoes, Hurricanes, Heat Waves, Snowstorms, Tsunamis, and Other Natural Disasters*. New York, NY: Palgrave Macmillan, 2012.

Timmer, Reed. *Into the Storm: Violent Tornadoes, Killer Hurricanes, and Death-Defying Adventures in Extreme Weather*. New York, NY: Dutton, 2010.

Ward, Peter Douglas. *The Flooded Earth: Our Future in a World Without Ice Caps*. New York, NY: Basic Books, 2010.

Index

About the Author

Alex David has her MFA from New England State College. She has written a series of books called *We the Weirdos*. Her poems and short stories have been published in literary journals such as *Green Mountains Review* and *Adelaide Literary Magazine*. Additionally, she has taught a class on eco-fiction at Canisius College in Buffalo, New York. She loves to learn and write about climate science. She is hopeful for the future.